Nature's Underground Wonderland

KARTCHNER

CAVERNS

BY SAM NEGRI

Photography by K.L. Day and Arizona Conservation Projects. Additional photography by Princely Nesadurai on page 5 and by David Elms on pages 1, 6, 8, 9, 12 (bottom), 14, 16-17, 25, and 29.

Prepared by the Book Division of *Arizona Highways* magazine, a monthly publication of the Arizona Department of Transportation.

Nina M. La France — Publisher
Bob Albano — Managing Editor
Robert J. Farrell and Evelyn Howell — Book Editors
Richard Maack — Photography Editor
Cindy Mackey — Production Director
Peter Ensenberger — Director of Photography

Mary Winkelman Velgos — Art Director
Russ Wall and Barbara Denney — Designers
Kevin Kibsey — Map Illustration
Ellen Straine — Production
Bonnie Trenga and Betty Campbell — Copy Editors

Library of Congress Catalog Number 97-76032   ISBN 0-916179-65-6

(COVER) This collage shows some of Kartchner's hanging stalactites overlaid by a site diagram of the cave. The diagram motif is repeated throughout the book.
(INSIDE FRONT COVER) Framed by rising stalagmites and icicle-like stalactites, a flowstone formation looks like a melting wedding cake. Kartchner Caverns is a significant find because it is a "living" cave — these mineral formations are still growing with each tiny drip of water.
(ABOVE) A special type of stalagmite on Kartchner's floor, called a "fried egg" for obvious reasons, looks gelatinous. However, the "egg yolk" is really rock, and it's just wet, not slimy.
(BACK COVER) Kubla Khan, the large central column, dwarfs an observer in the Throne Room. Almost 60 feet high, Kubla Khan is the highest known column in an Arizona cave.

Nature's
Underground
Wonderland

KARTCHNER
CAVERNS

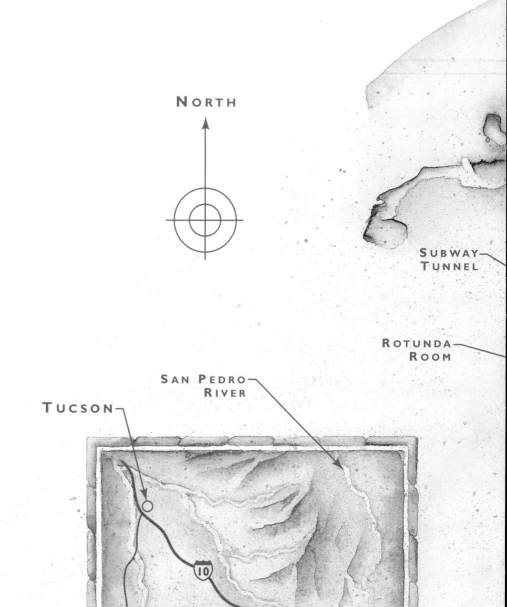

NORTH

SUBWAY
TUNNEL

ROTUNDA
ROOM

SAN PEDRO
RIVER

TUCSON

SANTA CRUZ
RIVER

WHETSTONE
MOUNTAINS

BENSON

KARTCHNER
CAVERNS

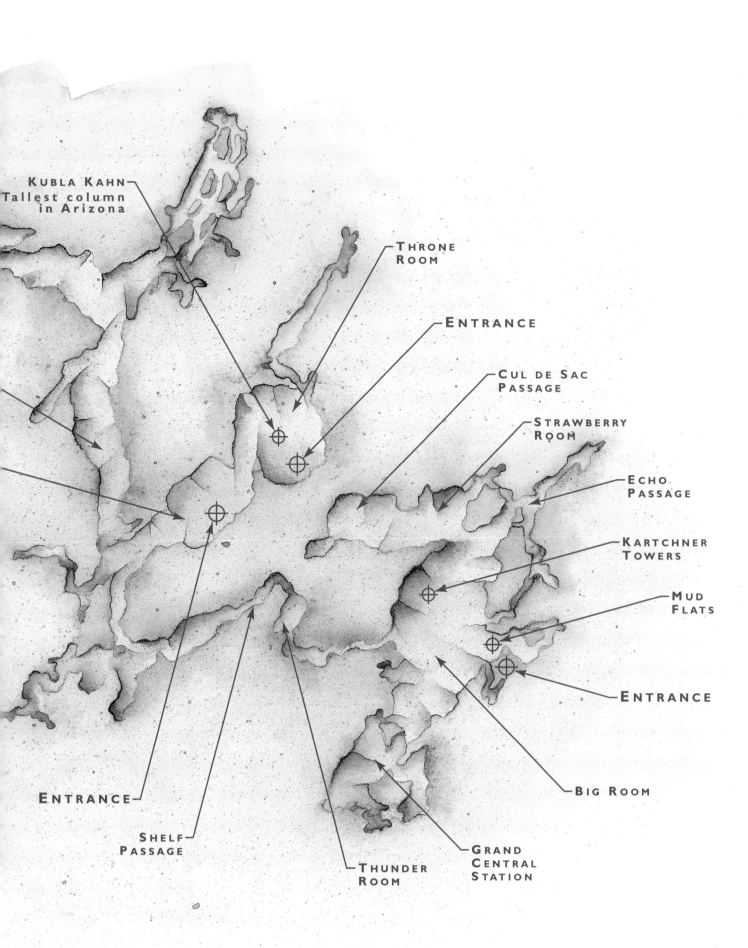

KUBLA KAHN
Tallest column
in Arizona

THRONE
ROOM

ENTRANCE

CUL DE SAC
PASSAGE

STRAWBERRY
ROOM

ECHO
PASSAGE

KARTCHNER
TOWERS

MUD
FLATS

ENTRANCE

BIG ROOM

ENTRANCE

SHELF
PASSAGE

THUNDER
ROOM

GRAND
CENTRAL
STATION

Basic chemical reactions have been the architect of this underground landscape. Those reactions first hollowed out the limestone base and are now filling it with stalactites, "soda straws," helictites, rimstone dams, and calcite "shields." Even the cave walls lacking these otherworldly formations are stained with incredibly beautiful mineral tapestries of reds, blue-greens, and browns, grays, and whites.

Before we can go "down under," there are safety items to be checked. Park rangers remind us of the procedures to protect not only ourselves but also the delicate features that we'll be passing. Some of them, called speleothems, are so fragile that a careless touch can ruin thousands of years of growth.

It's finally time to descend the 40-foot-long shaft and enter Kartchner. We make our way down and go through an air-lock door. A short crawl through the first chamber and we stand up in the "big room"; it's as beautiful as I remembered it.

Nearby, shadows hide behind stalactites as we move by with our headlamps. The bobbing of our heads as we walk makes the shadows dance.

A short distance away is complete darkness. Our light is absorbed by the void, and what may be a hundred yards to the outer wall could just as well be a hundred miles. I think back upon the first two visitors and marvel at what it must have been like the first few years while the cave was being mapped.

We decide to break up into two smaller groups, one going to explore areas for future photography while the other, mine, gets to be more leisurely and discuss some of the more technical challenges in opening this cave.

get up on the morning of my second trip into Kartchner Caverns and feel as though it is my birthday. It's that happy feeling that gifts await you just for being there. I notice my companions can't help but smile their version of my smile.

When Randy Tufts and Gary Tenen first ventured into the cave in 1974, there were no human footprints, and they swore themselves to secrecy for protection's sake. Imagine. There were footprints on the moon before there were footprints in Kartchner. When the discovery was announced to the world 14 years later and the caverns became an Arizona state park, newspaper editorials stated that Tufts and Tenen had the "uncommon good sense not to blab their news to the world" until the cave was assured of protection.

Kartchner Caverns, in southern Arizona halfway between Benson and Sierra Vista on State Route 90, was named after the family who owned the land (and helped protect the cave). It is a striking contrast to the surrounding desert landscape. Along the 2.4 miles of surveyed passageways are two large rooms, each about 100 feet high and a football field long. Kartchner has all the ingredients of a subtropical rain forest except the most important: the light of the sun.

(ABOVE)
A heavy calcite shield looms over rounded stalagmites below.

There are many challenges to be addressed in developing and operating Kartchner Caverns. Because humidity is almost 100 percent and it's 68° F just below the surface of the desert, we need to ensure that we don't dry out the cave when we open it to the public.

Lighting is particularly tricky. People will bring in spores on their clothing, and the light we add along the paths could trigger growth. Keep the lights too low, however, and visitors will stumble.

In addition, how do you get people close enough to the formations so they can fully appreciate their beauty, but at the same time not so close that a curious hand will damage them?

What's more, it is anticipated that people will come from around the world to visit this splendid place. To protect the cave we will have to communicate in a variety of languages the need for extreme caution during the visits.

The list of issues to be handled seems endless. How do you protect the small colony of bats found here in summer? How large should a group tour be; and how long should it take? What color lights do we use for display purposes? Can we develop a cave trail without stairs that allows complete access for the disabled visitor?

As we sit and discuss some of these things, we notice that the other group is returning. We can't yet hear them, but we see an occasional flicker of light in the distance. We gather once again and make a short trip to the "strawberry room" and another to the "echo passage." It is very tempting to name everything that you see, but we try to resist that temptation for two reasons. First, we think that your imagination is every bit as fertile as ours. When you visit, we don't want to take away one of the real joys of Kartchner: It is so highly decorated that you are sure to find something you'll want to name yourself.

Second, other cave owners have told us that naming features dates a cavern to its discovery and sometimes those names lose their meaning. Cave owners have shown me their biggest embarrassments, and most often they are names they wish they could retrieve from the public mind.

As we make our way back to the shaft, we slow down, partly because crawling and stooping for the last four hours in an atmosphere of 100 percent humidity is taking its toll. But also we know that we're headed back, and we don't want to leave — there might be one more beautiful stalactite or helictite that we don't want to miss.

A short while later we are out on top again, getting into cleaner clothing and putting away our equipment.

I think back to my youth when I went on a hunting trip with my grandfather. It was the first time I was allowed to go into the woods on my own. I found a large English walnut tree to sit under and, thinking youthful thoughts, wondered if anyone had ever sat there before. Looking down, I noticed a discarded tin can. I have wondered ever since if there was anyplace left on earth that man hadn't ruined with disrespect. Kartchner Caverns is such a place, a present that will keep me smiling for a lifetime.

KEN TRAVOUS
DIRECTOR, ARIZONA STATE PARKS

SECRECY AND INTRIGUE LEAD TO A STATE PARK

James Kartchner may have been the first to notice something a little unusual about the hills containing the cave that now bears his name. Kartchner was an educator and a rancher in St. David, a small town east of the Whetstone Mountains, in south-eastern Arizona. Whenever he and his sons would ride the hills to check on their cattle, their horses' hoofs made a peculiar sound on the limestone rock. "You know," Kartchner commented to his sons, "it sounds like these hills are hollow."

Kartchner had bought land in the Whetstones, about 40 miles southeast of Tucson, in 1942. It would be another 32 years before he or anyone else would discover just how hollow the hills were.

(ABOVE) As rainwater drips through the cave's limestone roof, it dissolves various minerals and deposits them slowly, sometimes forming rows of stalactites and tiny, twisting helictites like these.

Various spelunkers, amateur cave explorers, had poked around the Whetstones hoping to find a new cave. Cavers look for certain telltale clues. If the area contains limestone, it may also contain caves because limestone dissolves when water seeps through it, forming underground cavities. Sinkholes are another good sign. A sinkhole is a depression in the ground created when these cavities collapse. The Whetstones have the most extensive limestone deposits in southern Arizona and are riddled with sinkholes. But until 1974 no one had ever found a cave worth talking about. Or, as we shall see, worth *not* talking about.

In 1966 Randy Tufts, a Tucson native with an insatiable curiosity about caves, started making regular trips to the Whetstone Mountains looking, as he put it, "for a cave no one had ever found." At

Photography by David Elms (page 6) and K.L. Day and Arizona Conservation Projects (page 7).

Part of the Big Room, the jagged ceiling and spiked floor shown here are a fraction of an area that is about as long as a football field.

Water droplets bead the tips of translucent rock tubes called "soda straws." The larger, surrounding stalactites, nicknamed "carrots," formed when soda straws clogged, and the mineralized solution poured down the sides.

that time one of the few decent roads into the Whetstones went up Middle Canyon, passing the Lone Star fluorite mine, located within the Coronado National Forest directly west of the Kartchners' property. After making about a dozen trips into the range, Tufts had met with little success. Finally, on one trip, out of frustration he stopped at the Lone Star Mine and asked one of the miners if he knew of any caves in the area. To his surprise the miner said yes, there was a cave nearby.

"Some high school kids got into it. They had to squeeze through a tight spot to do it," he said. According to the miner, the cave was located somewhere in the limestone knolls that Tufts had been driving by each time he went exploring in the Whetstones.

A week later Tufts went back to the area with two friends and his uncle. They spent most of the day hiking around the limestone knolls and eventually located a sinkhole and an opening that led into a small chamber. There was a narrow crack along one wall and they looked to see whether it might lead deeper in. They could determine nothing

and, feeling the boulders near the crack were unstable, they decided to leave. The chamber, they concluded, was just another dusty dry hole that wasn't worth pursuing. However, Tufts marked the hole on his topographic map.

For the next seven years, he was too absorbed with his

studies at the University of Arizona, where he was a geology student, to do much caving. In 1970 he met Gary Tenen at a political gathering and the two became friends. Tenen was the cook at a popular campus coffeehouse and Tufts became his assistant. A year later, when they were still students, the two moved into an apartment with a mutual friend.

(ABOVE) When spelunkers Randy Tufts (left) and Gary Tenen (right) discovered Kartchner Caverns in 1974, they noticed the lack of footprints. Three-fourths of the cavern floors have never been walked on, even during continuous exploration.

Tenen knew of Tufts' interest in caving, but he had never tried it. Because of his own interest in science — he was an entomology student — he asked Tufts to take him on one of his caving excursions. Their first trip was to a cave in the Huachuca Mountains, south of the Whetstones, and even though it was a heavily vandalized cave, the experience was enough to whet Tenen's appetite for caving. His enthusiasm rekindled Tufts' interest in caving, and before long the two were out scouring the vacant hills south and east of Tucson. In the fall of 1974 Tufts went back to the Whetstones with another friend, a non-caver. He quickly located the sinkhole at the spot he had marked earlier. However, this time, walking near a stream on the southern side of the hill, they found a horizontal hole some 60 yards from the sinkhole. Tufts wondered if the presence of the two openings meant there were cave passages between them. When he returned to Tucson, he told Tenen about his theory, and the two agreed to return the next weekend to do some exploring.

This view is into the immense Big Room with its forest of stalactites. The reddish formation above the observer's right shoulder is "cave bacon," colored by deposits of iron oxide.

On a cool November afternoon they went back. First they explored the horizontal entrance, but concluded that major excavation would be needed to get into it any deeper than 30 feet. They decided to take a look at the opening on the other side, in the sinkhole, even though Tufts had checked it seven years earlier and found nothing. They squirmed into the chamber, and Tufts remarked that although everything looked more or less as he remembered it, something seemed different.

"This time the air was moving. There was a breeze coming up from between the rocks, through a crack. Not just any breeze. It was warm, moist, and smelled like bat guano. This was new and compelling evidence," Tufts said. The fact that it was a cool November day no doubt made a difference. On the previous trip he hadn't felt the warm breeze from the cave because he had been there in warmer weather. "The cave wasn't breathing," he observed.

Encouraged, the two twisted their way down through the crack. Five feet below, and not visible from above, was a chamber about the size of an average living room. They soon saw unmistakable evidence — footprints and broken stalactites — that others had been this far before. A crawl space led from the first "room" to a second small room. But, neither of the rooms, they concluded, were large enough to account for the breeze. Only a sizable cave could produce it, but where was it coming from?

After inspecting every square inch of the two rooms, they discovered a crawl-way at the floor level in the second room. It was about 10 inches high and two feet across. There was no doubt the breeze was coming from that hole. Tufts squirmed into it, inching forward about 20 feet until the tunnel came to an abrupt end against a rock barrier. However, in the middle of the barrier there was a hole, a six-inch oval. A damp wind blew through the small blowhole. Tufts tried to peer through the opening, but the wind kept blowing out his carbide light.

This was the kind of moment that stirs a caver's blood. Something was definitely behind that small fissure, but what could it be? The question cavers often ask when they find a new passage is, "Does it go?" meaning, does this lead anywhere or will it be

(ABOVE) A mud-soaked caver enters the Throne Room. Until the new tunnel was completed in 1997, visitors spent two to three hours crawling the half mile from the Big Room to the Rotunda. They went on all fours through cold mud and, if the passage was flooded, chin-deep water.

(BELOW LEFT) A calcite shield is fluted with mineral draperies.
(BELOW RIGHT) A visitor looks up at a section of ceiling
heavily spiked with stalactites. Glistening with moisture, the
rounded formations beside him are rocky debris covered
with flowstone, minerals deposited by sheets of water.

Photography by K.L. Day and Arizona Conservation Projects (pages 12–13, top and page 13, bottom) and David Elms (page 12, bottom).

another dead end? Clearly, this hole went someplace, but where? With the thrill of discovery propelling them, Tufts and Tenen went to work with an eight-pound sledgehammer, taking turns chipping away at the limestone bedrock until the hole was barely large enough for a person to squeeze through.

Tenen, the smaller of the two, is 5 feet 7 inches tall and then weighed 130 pounds. He'd practiced for tight spots like this one by wiggling through ordinary coat hangers. Tufts, who is 6 feet tall and weighed 170 pounds, had to remove his shirt and exhale to make it through the opening. "It was like being born all over again," he remarked.

After the blowhole, the passage became slightly higher. They were able to crawl on hands and knees on a floor carpeted with bat guano and hackberry seeds. There was no sign on the walls or the floor that any human being had ever been there. Some 50 feet ahead of them they could see only darkness. They crawled toward that space and found themselves in a 10-foot-high corridor that took off in two directions. They were able to walk upright for the next 300 feet. Around them, in the jerky light of their headlamps, the chamber glistened with stalactites, soda straws (stalactites the thickness of a drinking straw), and tiny twisted fingers of calcite called helictites. They walked gingerly, taking care not to touch or damage anything.

They continued a bit farther on that first trip, but neither knew how far they had gone. What they knew beyond a doubt was that they had violated one of the first rules of caving. They had not informed anyone of their whereabouts. Cavers typically leave information with someone at home, and almost always they travel in fours, so that if someone is in trouble, one can stay with the injured person and two can climb out for help. Tufts and Tenen were on their own. They could have been buried alive and no one would ever know what had become of them.

It was a sobering thought, so they stopped and carefully retraced their steps, giddy with the thrill of the amazing world they had stumbled into. It was every caver's dream: an untouched, living cave, elaborately decorated with formations that were still growing. It was a subterranean jewel box that had taken about a million years to form, and no other humans had ever set foot inside it.

Tufts was born in 1948; Tenen in 1951. In 1974 they were still young men, and suddenly they were young men with a problem. They had done enough caving in southern Arizona to know that once word of a new find slipped out, hordes of curious individuals would descend on the cave. Before long, the great untouched gallery would be destroyed by graffiti and litter, desecrated by souvenir hunters taking home bits of stalactites and other formations that had been growing in the darkness for a million years.

They believed that, since they had discovered the cave, it was their responsibility to protect it. Making matters worse, the cave was simply too accessible. It was only a half mile off a paved state route and a mere eight miles south of a major interstate highway. From the cave's entrance, traffic could be heard clearly.

But what were they to do? For safety's sake and to avoid the publicity that would inevitably result if a public rescue were necessary, they had to bring others into the picture. At first these were a few friends who were athletic but not cavers and thus unlikely to return on their own. Among these was their roommate, Steve Northway, who provided the cave's first —but certainly not its last— name. Northway couldn't fit into the first crack to get into the cave, so he sat outside and waited, and when the others emerged, he suggested they call the place "Xanadu," the terrestrial paradise Samuel Taylor Coleridge invented in his famous poem, *Kubla Khan*: "In Xanadu did Kubla Khan / A stately pleasure-dome decree..."

It took a full year of exploration before Tufts and Tenen knew the full extent of what they had discovered. What they had crawled into that November day turned out to be the entrance to a cave two-and-a-half miles long, containing two large rooms. If the "breakdown" or fallen rock were removed, each of the rooms would be roughly the size of a football field. Off the two main rooms were 26 smaller ones, almost all of them dripping with rock formations that looked like something created by a Hollywood special effects artist, only all of this was natural.

To preserve the cave, they marked their trails and placed many areas off-limits. They took care not to

Rock formations decorate a curve of ceiling only where faults and fissures in the stone allow water to seep through, building the tiny soda straws and draping the mounded column with dissolved limestone.

touch anything. If they accidentally broke a formation, they glued it back together with dental cement. Not wanting to leave footprints in some sensitive passages, they removed their shoes and walked in their socks. "We did not treat Xanadu as a recreational cave," Tenen noted. "Once we concluded we had found all of it, we stopped going."

A few friends and cavers knew what they had found, though all were sworn to secrecy. Numerous relatives and friends were simply not told. The guiding principle was that only those "who needed to know" for safety's sake, or to continue exploration, would be told. When dealing with strangers, they adopted aliases for themselves and deliberately steered attention away from the Whetstones.

After the initial burst of exhilaration over their find, Tufts and Tenen were in a quandary. How could such an accessible cave be kept a secret and kept in its pristine condition? Inevitably, someone

Photography by David Elms (page 14 and pages (6-17) and K.L. Day and Arizona Conservation Projects (page 15).

else would discover it, they felt. Who would they be and how would they treat their find? After much thought, they settled on what Tufts called "a paradoxical notion": Why not protect the cave by developing it as a commercial attraction?

In 1977 Tufts visited various developed caves to see how Xanadu compared. He returned and told Tenen that Xanadu was as good or better than other tourist caves. "We thought if it had economic value, someone would supervise it and protect it," Tenen said. Briefly, the two considered buying the land and developing the cave themselves, but neither of them had the money.

When they first explored the cave, they didn't know it was on private land — a mistake that's easy to make in Arizona, where hills and mountains are often a patchwork of state, federal, and private land. This land, they soon discovered, was owned by James and Lois Kartchner of St. David. But who were the

In the Strawberry Room, the pinkish cast to these formations is from the degree of iron oxide deposited. To the left is the shoulder of a large formation nicknamed "Strawberry Shortcake."

Kartchners and what were they like? How would they react if they were told about the cave?

In the many years since 1978, when Tufts and Tenen approached James Kartchner in his front yard, they have repeatedly commented on the cave's good fortune. Kartchner, who died in 1986, had been a science teacher and the superintendent of schools in St. David. He and Lois had 10 children of their own and two that they adopted. Six of their children are medical doctors, and one has a Ph.D.

Tenen, an avid photographer, had taken numerous slides of the cave's formations. He and Tufts had prepared a script and planned to divulge their find gradually, only after they had gauged the Kartchners' attitude. They quickly realized James Kartchner was at least as interested in geology and related matters as they were, and the script went out the window. Tenen set up his slides, cautioning his host about the need for secrecy.

About two months later, when Kartchner was 78, he and five of his sons accompanied Tufts and Tenen on a tour of the cave to determine its potential for development. The discoverers hoped the family would see the need for protection. In this case they needn't have worried.

"We were in complete disbelief at the size and beauty of it," said Max Kartchner, an anesthesiologist who lives in Benson. "It was almost a sacred experience, so exquisite and out of this world."

After their trip into the cave, the family asked Tufts and Tenen to prepare a proposal outlining the best options for protecting it, so the two then set out to learn as much as they could about how trails and lighting could be installed in a cave without damaging the natural resource. Using money from a joint bank account they had set up with the Kartchners, and determined to keep their activities secret, they adopted new aliases and hired Jan and Orion Knox, a couple from Austin, Texas, to map the cave.

Tenen used the name Mike Lewis. Tufts became Bob Clark. It was an amusing coincidence, they realized later, that their new names were Lewis and Clark, like the two explorers who had made the scientific survey of much of western North America from 1803 to 1806.

Near the main trail, the ceiling's arch opens into the Big Room, where the roof peaks at 55 feet. The ceiling in the Throne Room, Kartchner's other large chamber, reaches about 70 feet at its highest point.

Tenen used his alias when he attended two conventions of the National Caves Association and when he worked for five months as a volunteer at Caverns of Sonora in Texas and at Luray Caverns in Virginia. He paid for everything with cash to avoid using checks or credit cards that showed his real name.

The elaborate ruse was necessary because the national caving community was tight-knit. Information and rumors could spread rapidly. Since cavers sometimes become identified with mountain ranges they explored, Tufts and Tenen feared that if they used their real names, the word would get out that they had found something in the Whetstones. Anyone they told about the cave, except the Kartchners and, later, Bruce Babbitt, then governor of Arizona, was required to sign a secrecy agreement, threatening "theological punishment" to anyone who divulged the cave's location or even its existence.

Nevertheless, some leaks occurred. One of them led to a scene that could have come straight out of an old western movie. Steve Holland, a caver and acquaintance of Tenen, overheard a group planning a trip to the Whetstones to search for a rumored cave on the Kartchner land. He informed Tenen, and a plan was devised. Holland would wrangle an invitation to go along with the other four cavers. "I became a mole," he said. He told Tenen when the group was going to be at the cave. Tenen contacted the Kartchners to arrange a confrontation that would scare off the interlopers.

A few months later, the five cavers showed up at the site to excavate the horizontal entrance that Tufts and Tenen had originally abandoned as impenetrable. A few minutes after their arrival, three Kartchner brothers,

(ABOVE) A close-up look at some rootlike helictites. Appearing almost fibrous, they are hardened mineral like all the cave formations. (RIGHT) Tightly clustered stalactites hover over blockier stalagmites.

Paul, Rex, and Fred, rode up on horseback, one of them with a pistol dangling from his side. "What are you doing on our land?" one of them asked the group.

Holland pretended to be as shocked as the other cavers. "The Kartchners acted like rough and tough ranchers, even though one of them was an anesthesiologist and another a teacher," he recalled. They took down the names of the interlopers, told them they were trespassing, and warned them they would be arrested if they were ever found there again.

After about two years, the Kartchners decided the cost of developing the cave themselves was prohibitive. However, along with Tufts and Tenen, they continued to guard the cave. Finally, in 1984, Tufts and Tenen came up with an alternative: Maybe the state would be interested in purchasing the site to develop it as a state park.

The discoverers approached Governor Babbitt. The governor was interested, but wanted to see the cave for himself. Babbitt, who had a background in geology before he became a lawyer, toured the cave in April, 1985. He brought along his sons, Chris, 10, and T.J., 8, first making them promise they would keep it a secret. He also lectured them on not touching anything and following directions carefully.

"After this great lecture, the only person who knocked over a stalagmite was me," the governor said. "We were climbing up an incline and my heel knocked over a baby stalagmite. My kids have never let me forget it."

Impressed with what he saw, Babbitt threw his

support behind the clandestine movement to get the cave into public ownership. One of the biggest problems involved the business of obtaining an appraisal of the property and guiding the project through the legislative process without attracting publicity and jeopardizing the site.

It took three more years, two more governors, two more state parks directors, and some tense, behind-the-scenes political maneuvering before the state bought the cave. Everyone involved was so consumed with the need for secrecy that State Parks Director Ken Travous asked legislative leaders to write a bill authorizing the cave's purchase but to obscure the bill's language so that no one would know exactly what was being purchased until the day of the vote. Senate Bill 1188 was essentially dummy legislation that made no mention of the cave. Its original wording dealt with routine accounting changes within the parks department. Until the final vote, only six members of the legislature knew that the dummy legislation actually authorized the state to buy the cave and the land around it for $1,625,000.

The day the bill was passed, April 27, 1988, its language was changed to clearly authorize the creation of James and Lois Kartchner Caverns State Park. The State Senate approved the measure by a vote of 27-0; the House by a vote of 52-4. Fourteen years of protective secrecy came to an abrupt end, and the cave and new park were announced to the public.

While the discovery of the cave and the elaborate

(LEFT) Crouched beneath a stony vault, a visitor looks at a backlit slab of "cave bacon." The corrugated upright spire is a stalagmite. (BELOW) A set of small "fried eggs" cluster on the cave floor. When it comes to giving nicknames, cavers often seem to have food on their minds.

secrecy were remarkable, the steps that followed were just as significant. Almost immediately after the park was established, Travous put together a team of nationally known cave experts to study everything in the cave and everything outside that might impact the interior. Ron Bridgemon, former president of the Cave Research Foundation, an organization that studies caves throughout the United States, said that, to his knowledge, scientific studies had never before been done prior to developing a cave as a tourist attraction.

"These studies are usually done after the cave has opened [to the public] and something has been messed up," he said. "Then they go back in and try to fix it. What the state is doing with Kartchner is unique."

In addition, experts in designing cave tours were recruited to supervise the underground construction and development. Extraordinary care was taken in the development, both above and below ground, to keep the cave in good condition.

Kartchner Caverns became a state park so that it could be preserved and protected and used as a living classroom where the public could learn something about earth sciences and the fragile life of a cave environment. For Tufts and Tenen, the creation of the park was like an investment from which all other caves might profit once the public saw its remarkable features and learned the necessity of preserving it and other caves for future generations.

ARTISTRY IN STONE

How Nature Created Kartchner Caverns

"Look closely. Can you see that droplet of water?"

The speaker was Randy Tufts. We were standing in his living room in Tucson in November, 1996. Kartchner Caverns had not yet opened as Arizona's 25th state park. We were talking about how the formations in the cave started from a single drop of water.

Tufts stepped over to a photograph on the wall showing a cave wall in Kartchner Caverns. It looked like a textured drape with muted colors forming bands that dropped in a more or less diagonal pattern. Tufts pointed to a bright spot that seemed suspended in the blackness to the left of the wall.

(ABOVE) Looking as appetizing as a real strip of bacon, mineral slabs like this are typically an eighth of an inch thick.
(OPPOSITE) In the main passage of the Big Room, a visitor stands in front of ridged draperies capped by flowstone.

The image, he knew, was not merely a photo of a rock and some moisture, but a picture of a process at work. The tiny droplet in the photo had just fallen from the end of something called a soda straw, a narrow, glass-like tube of rock hanging from the cave's ceiling.

The droplet of water seeped through the limestone, picking up calcium carbonate as it traveled; when the water hit the air in the cave, a chemical transformation occurred that eventually created the soda straw. The fragile soda straw, if it doesn't break under its own weight or get destroyed by someone colliding with it, will eventually grow into a stalactite, but that process will take thousands of years.

Typically, most stalactites and stalagmites grow only one-tenth of a millimeter per year, which is

Photography by K.L. Day and Arizona Conservation Projects (both pages).

Photography by K.L. Day and Arizona Conservation Projects (page 24 and pages 26-27) and David Elms (page 25).

(LEFT) Delicate soda straws build slowly until they break under their own weight. Sticking up from the mud, such fragments have been undisturbed for perhaps 20,000 years.
(ABOVE) Portions of Kartchner Caverns flood periodically, an important natural process for maintaining the cave's humidity. As water recedes, the mud acts as a humidity bank.

thinner than a strand of human hair. Having studied the buildup of these calcite deposits on primitive tools found in other caves, scientists estimate it would take more than 750 years to accumulate one inch. However, 750 years in the life of a rock or a cave is like the blink of an eye compared to the millions of years it takes to prepare for the creation of that single inch. Before there can be a limestone cave, there must be limestone. Where did the limestone come from? How were the Whetstone Mountains formed? What forces were at work that created an underground cavern filled with so many exotic shapes and colors? The answers lie millions of years in the past.

Some 200 million years ago, compacted limestone, formed 150 million years earlier from ancient marine life, was propelled upward by the buckling of the earth's crust and occasional volcanoes. These upheavals formed mountains in the inland sea that once covered what is now Arizona. Later, movements in the tectonic plates under the earth created great cracks and fissures that allowed water to penetrate the limestone deposits in places like the Whetstone Mountains, creating, about one million years ago, the cave now called Kartchner Caverns.

Compared to granite or shale, limestone is a highly soluble rock. As rain falls, it combines with the air's carbon dioxide to form a weak carbonic acid solution, which seeps through millions of cracks in the mountain's surface and dissolves the limestone. In the final stages of this cave's development, the level of the underground water dropped, leaving open chambers in the limestone.

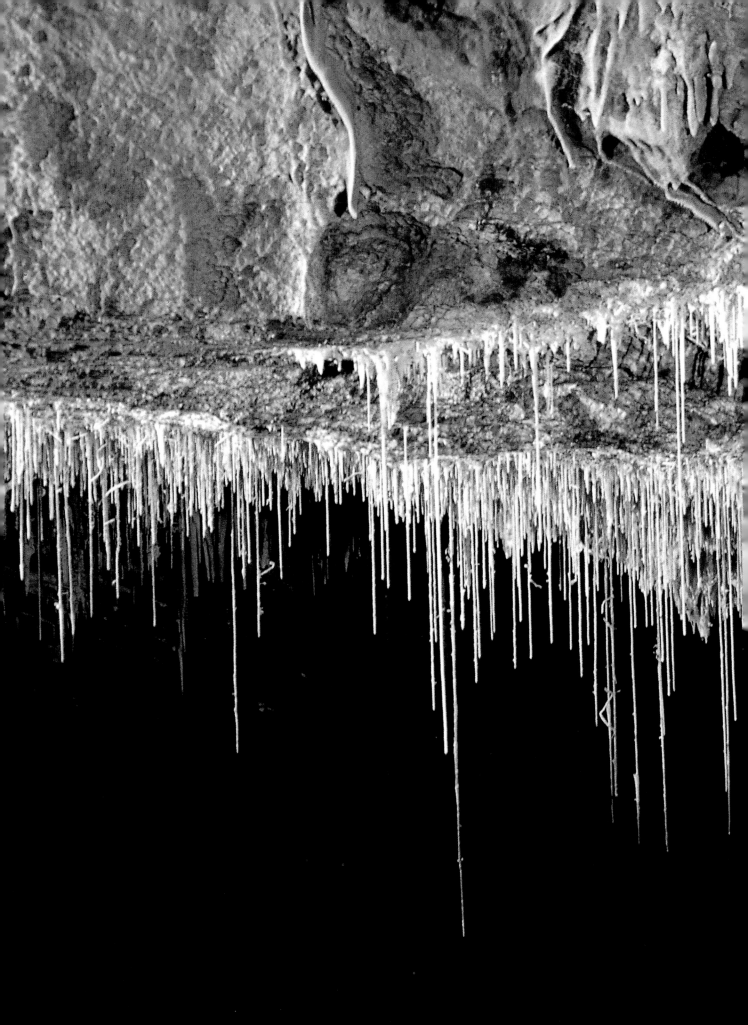

Soda straws, looking like filaments of spider silk, dangle from the ceiling of the Big Room.

The first drop of water to seep through the mountain's surface soils and reach that ancient cavity began the process of decorating Kartchner Caverns with the stunning variety of calcite formations visible today.

While the shapes and colors of the formations in Kartchner vary considerably, depending on minerals carried in the water and the trajectory of the water, the chemical process is the same. Acidic rainwater seeps underground and when it reaches an air-filled cave, it loses its carbon dioxide and crystallizes into calcium carbonate.

If we could speed up this process enough to watch it happening, we would see that each droplet of water, carrying its load of dissolved minerals, hangs from the ceiling before it drops to the floor. Even in that brief time, some of the carbon dioxide escapes from the water, causing a ring of calcium carbonate to form on the ceiling. Later, another droplet hangs from this spot, and in the same way it adds a layer of mineral to the ring.

After countless years of slow drip after drip, these rings form a hollow, straw-like cylinder. As the cylinder develops, droplets run down the inside as well as the outside and merge at the tip in a formation with the shape of an icicle, known as a stalactite. A similar process occurs on the floor of the cave. When the water droplet splashes on the floor, carbon dioxide escapes, leaving behind —

Geologists estimate that soda straws grow a tenth of an inch every century, depending on how much outside water seeps in.

because of the splash — an irregular layer of calcium carbonate, which eventually will grow into rough cylindrical formations. These formations rising from the cave's floor are known as stalagmites.

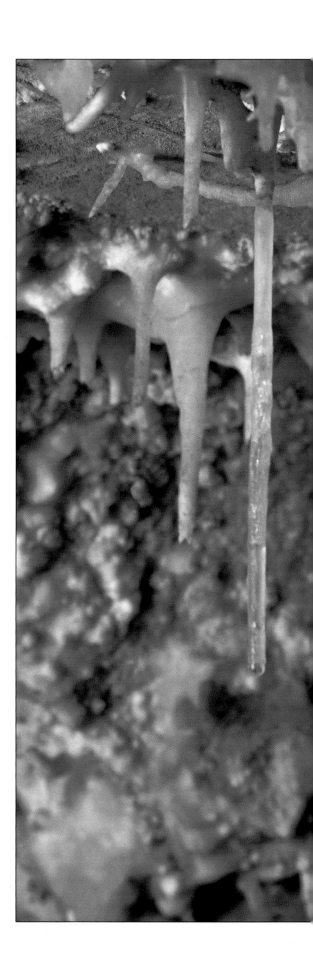

The process of making the cavity itself takes longer than making the formations, and geologists say the interesting thing about a place like Kartchner is that it may not be the final curtain call: Over time there may be changes in the chemistry and the formations, and as a result the formations can keep changing.

Kartchner is an almost pristine example of the whole process. Limestone caves are abundant, but, unlike Kartchner, most of them are inaccessible. The vast majority are also extremely small, although there are exceptions such as the chamber at Carlsbad Caverns, New Mexico, which is nearly a mile long and 350 feet high.

Throughout the dizzying network of boulders and narrow passageways in Kartchner, walls are decorated sporadically with an elaborate frieze consisting of curled and calcified limestone helictites, formed by water forcing its way through tiny fissures. Pale draperies or curtains — formed when trickling water deposits an undulating line of calcite on the underside of a sloping ceiling or wall — sometimes are striped with alternating layers of reddish brown bands (produced by various iron compounds) that look remarkably like large slabs of bacon. In fact these formations are called "cave bacon," and some spectacular examples can be seen in Kartchner. Other large deposits in the cave appear to be perfect sunny-side-up eggs, although their surfaces are smooth and hard.

(LEFT) Cave formations offer a menu of fantastic shapes and colors, yet they all start as dissolved minerals deposited by water. It may look like an icy waterfall, but this is a shield of rock. (BELOW) Mounded flowstone drips over limestone draperies, with tips of stalactites showing in the background.

Like Carlsbad, Kartchner Caverns is home to a population of bats. Between 1,000 and 2,000 insect-eating bats, most of them pregnant females, move into Kartchner's Big Room from May to September and raise their young. You may see or hear small bats in the upper reaches of the subterranean landscape, flitting among thin, coral-colored fingers that hang like drapes behind shallow pools of cool water.

Studies of the bat guano found in the Throne Room — where bats no longer live — show that they roosted there some 50,000 years ago. The bats are an important part of the life cycle of the cave. Their excrement acts as fertilizer, providing nutrients that enable other organisms to grow. These organisms have grown for thousands of years in complete darkness, an important consideration for preserving the cave in its original condition. Park designers, intent on keeping the cave functioning as naturally as possible, chose special lights for the cave that would not encourage the growth of algae or any of the other life forms that might be affected by a change in the light levels.

Kartchner is remarkable because it is a "wet" or "live" cave, meaning that the calcite formations are still growing. Though the terrain outside the cave is arid, the cave's relative humidity averages 99 percent all year. And while outside temperatures can reach

Photography by K.L. Day and Arizona Conservation Projects (both pages).

100° in the summer, the temperature inside the cave remains right around 67°. To minimize the damaging effects of the dry outside air on the cave formations, air locks have been installed. If the formations lose their moisture, they stop growing.

Other protective measures were devised to minimize the human impact: Visitors entering the cave first pass through an air curtain that blows lint from their clothing; then they go through an area where mist forces any remaining lint against their clothing. As if that were not enough, special kick plates were constructed along the trail inside the cave to collect any lint or other foreign materials that visitors may be carrying on their shoes and that may alter Kartchner's fragile ecosystem. All visitors are told not to touch anything because oil from their skin can cause a formation to stop growing.

As Tufts noted, "The quality and diversity of the formations in the cave are unusual. There's a little bit of everything in there, including a 50-foot-high column, a 30-foot-high stalagmite, and some rare formations called shields."

There's also a 21-foot-long, 2-inch-diameter soda straw hanging from the ceiling of the Throne Room, which, until a slightly longer one was found in Australia, was the longest formation of this type in the world.

"But," asks Tufts, "what is the key point about Kartchner? Not that it is beautiful nor that it will spur growth in Benson, but the fact that it is in excellent condition and is being kept that way for posterity. That's why it's attractive. There is great drama here. Can the cave be kept in good condition with the park as the vehicle? That was the theory . . . conserving the cave by developing it. A great paradox . . . requiring constant vigilance."

In addition to being an intriguing, living scientific laboratory, Kartchner Caverns enchant visitors because of the mystery that goes with a journey under the surface of the earth. Spelunkers who crawl into these unexplored worlds are sometimes compared to mountain climbers, perhaps because of their adventurous spirit, but Tufts points out a significant difference:

"The appeal of caving is that you do not know what you're going to find. Does the cave continue or is it another dead end? Finding and exploring a cave like this one is like being a sculptor who finds the form he is seeking in the stone he's working. But with a discovery of this kind comes a responsibility to protect it because caves are not a renewable resource. Once a formation that has been growing for a million years is broken, it's never coming back."

(ABOVE) The "bacon's" striped colors are determined by the various minerals deposited. (RIGHT) Sheets of water left these tiers of flowstone by cascading over breakdown debris from the Big Room's ceiling.

Photography by K.L. Day and Arizona Conservation Projects.